und.... your stress

{ *30 curiously fun ways*

to take off tension }

LOIS LEVY, M.S.

SOURCEBOOKS, INC.®
NAPERVILLE, ILLINOIS

Copyright © 2005, 1999 by Lois Levy
Cover and internal design © 2005 by Sourcebooks, Inc.
Cover photo © Veer Images

Sourcebooks and the colophon are registered trademarks of Sourcebooks, Inc.

Quotation sources:
Bartlett, John, *Familiar Quotations*, (Little, Brown & Co., Boston, 1980). Frank, Leonard
Roy, *Webster's Quotationary* (Random House, New York, 1999). Lamb, G.F., *Harrap's
Book of Humorous Quotations* (Harrap, London, 1990). Maggio, Rosalie, *The Beacon
Book of Quotations by Women* (Beacon Press, Boston, 1992). McWilliams, Peter, *Life 101
Quote Book* (Prelude Press, 1997). Partnow, Elaine, *The Quotable Woman 1800-1981*
(Facts on File, New York, 1982). Warren, Roz, *Women's Lip* (Sourcebooks, Naperville,
IL, 1998).

Published by Sourcebooks, Inc.
P.O. Box 4410 Naperville, IL 60566
630-961-3900 Fax: 630-961-2168

ISBN: 1-4022-0532-5

First edition published in 1999.

The Library of Congress has catalogued the first edition as follows:
Levy, Lois B.
   Undress Your Stress: 30 curiously Fun ways to take off tension/
by Lois B. Levy
        p.   cm.
   1.Stress (Psychology) 2. Stress management. I. Title
BF575.S75.L47 1999
155.9'042--dc21 5   99-36917
                                                  CIP

Printed and bound in Canada
WC 10 9 8 7 6 5 4 3 2 1

To Kenny, without whom nothing happens.

acknowledgments

It's a pleasure to be able to say a public thank you to all the people who helped birth this book. Of course, I'll forget someone and to that person I say, "Please forgive me. It wasn't intentional. My memory isn't what it used to be."

First, I must salute my friend Connie Cordaro, who said, "Hey, this is a book," before it ever occurred to me that it could be. Then there's my cousin Rhoda who's been saying, "Please write a book," for about fifteen years.

I want to thank my son for not laughing at me when he heard what I was doing and for editing the raw material with wisdom and grace. He's a great supporter and my favorite moment of truth. He's taught me to laugh and to cry and to understand why a balanced life is sensible.

To Jane Ford for the perfect market survey. To Kaitryn and Steven Wertz for applauding the rough draft when I was most vulnerable. To all of the friends and colleagues who were willing to take a look and make comments.

To Deb Werksman, my editor, for making the process so easy and for being so enthusiastic about the project from the first minute.

To Kenny Kesslin who sat still and quiet for days on end so I would find the discipline to sit at the keyboard for hours at a time. This book is the outcome of his willingness always to be there for me.

And finally to my parents. It is the combination of their genetic material that gives me my sight, my intensity, my intelligence, my determination, my stubbornness, and my humor. At their table I grew up watching people who knew how to work, knew how to play, and didn't forget either.

table of contents

Foreword ix
Take Off the Tension 1
Laugh 7
   Major Hysterics 7
   The Fake Smile 10
   The Mirror Smile 12
Quiet Time 15
   Meditate 15
   Breathe Well 20
   Write 25
   Take a Bath 28
Noisy Time 31
   Groan 31
   Scream 32
   Sing 34
   Cry 36
Move Around 41
   Exercise 41
   Yoga 45
   Dance 49

Kindergarten Magic. **53**
   Read Aloud. 53
   Color and Cut. 56
Talk. **59**
   With Someone Else 59
   With Yourself. 62
   Prayer. 64
Escape **67**
   Waste Time. 67
   Go Outside. 69
   Go Home 72
   Go Away 73
Sleep **77**
   Get Enough 77
   Take a Nap 81
Stop The Madness. **83**
   Television. 83
   Sugar and Caffeine 86
   Stuff 90
   Worry. 92
   Take Your Pick. 94
The Power of Happiness. **99**
An Attitude of Gratitude **103**
The Last Hurrah **107**

foreword

So many of us slog through life wearing our angst, our anxiety, our exhaustion as if they were Easter outfits. It looks like we think it's some kind of fashion statement. Trust me, it isn't. To make a real statement, how about dressing up in joy or happiness or passion? It's time to undress our stress and clad ourselves in contentment.

Here's my pledge to you. If you pick just one activity from this book and do it consistently for the next three weeks, you will feel better. I guarantee it.

This is a book about taking care of yourself. It's something most of us don't do very well. Do you? Admit it—it's last on your list of things to do that never get done. But now you've noticed how depleted you feel physically and mentally, and something about this book called to you. That's a great first step.

In the 1950s, they promised us that by the 1990s we'd all be working twenty-hour weeks and our biggest problem would be all the leisure time we'd have. Somehow, the technology that was supposed to create all this leisure time for us has done exactly the opposite. We work more hours, have fewer resources, and we spend all of our time trying to do more and more faster and faster. Instead of more leisure time, most of us have less. When we do have some free time, we try to cram as much as we can into it. When was the last time you sat and looked out the window and just day-dreamed? Or walked slowly by a stream or watched the clouds roll by? We have to make space in our lives just to "be."

As a child of the 1950s, I've been waiting for all of this "down" time to magically appear in my life. It hasn't happened for me. Has it happened for you? I've been wondering what I'm doing wrong, but I've noticed that it isn't just me. It's most of us. And, as a self-employed person with a grown child, I have much more control over my life than most people do. So, if I feel overwhelmed by my schedule and all I have to do, that's not a good sign for the rest of you.

The good news is that everything contained in this small volume is easily doable, simple, fast, and cheap. The bad news is that I can't do any of it for you.

{ "If you are all wrapped up in yourself, you are overdressed." }

~Kate Halverson

take off the tension

Stress, according to *Webster's Dictionary,* is "a state of bodily or mental tension resulting from factors that tend to alter an existent equilibrium." Originally, stress was a metallurgy term about the force one inanimate object exerted against another. Today, when we talk about stress we're talking about people.

We are not designed physically to keep up with the technology we are smart enough to invent. Biologically, we are still quite primitive and our reactions to stressful situations are exactly the same as those of our original ancestors. Our bodies respond to stress by pumping adrenaline into our systems as a way to prepare for "fight or flight." Our muscles tense, we are ready to fight or flee for our very lives.

Unfortunately, that response was created for things like saber tooth tigers, not a slow ATM machine or the person with fifteen items in the twelve-item line. The physical response is designed to give us the best possible chance of survival in a dangerous situation. "Fight or flight" was not intended as a response to the fax machine getting stuck. But, it's the only physical response we have for stress and so instead of using it sparingly as our ancestors did, we find ourselves having small stress reactions all day long.

As technology continues to speed up our lives, we become more and more stressed because we are unable physically to go as fast as our machines would allow. Yet, we try and try to keep up, only to fall further behind, feeling more exhausted, and wondering what's wrong with us.

There's nothing wrong with us at all. We just aren't equipped to keep up with the machines. And it's time for us to stop trying.

We live in a nanosecond world and it's taking a toll on our bodies and our minds. When adrenaline is constantly being pushed through our systems, we wind up on an endocrine seesaw. First we're wired and then we crash. Each of us is going to have to take responsibility for finding "slow" places for ourselves.

Sometimes I go to the bank and stand in line just to remind myself of what it used to be like before ATMs and drive-thrus. It can be very communal and quite soothing as I stand waiting for a teller. I chat with other people in line or daydream. When there was no alternative, the bank line was a little piece of time out. So was my car. So was an airplane. Not anymore. With car phones, cellular phones, data hook-ups, fax machines, voice mail, and email, we can now keep going one hundred miles an hour no matter where we are. Those uncontrollable minutes or hours of respite no longer exist. You have to make them.

You have to protect your mind and your body by finding places in your life to be "old fashioned" and do things the old, slow way. Because our bodies can't cope with what technology has given us, each of us will have to take a stand in our own way.

Try washing the dishes by hand with someone you like, while playing soft music in the background. Rake the leaves with a real rake and not one of those horrid leaf-blower things. Reconnect with the natural rhythm of your body and see how it quiets and rests your mind as well.

This book will teach you specific techniques that range from a few seconds to thirty minutes. Most will take you five minutes or less. These are simple ways to create a "time out" for yourself during the day. The only real answer to the breakneck pace of life today is to slow down your own life. No one will do it for you and no one will help you do it. But you can do it for yourself. Since the technology is only going to get faster and it's never going to be like the "old" days, I share with you the things that can make a significant difference in your life. They are easy, quick, and don't require a lot of heavy, fancy, or expensive equipment. Most of these techniques can be done anywhere, any time, wearing any outfit.

Take your life back, five minutes at a time. You can do it.

"Not a shred of evidence
exists in favor of the idea
that life is serious."

~Brendan Gill

laugh

"Laughing is the fire-works of the soul."

~Josh Billings

Major Hysterics

When was the last time you laughed? No, I don't mean that fake thing you do at work or that giggly thing you do when you're telling a story. I mean a good, deep, belly laugh where you got red in the face and pounded the floor. Remember how great it made you feel?

Laughter is good for us. Norman Cousins laughed his way to a healthy body when the medical community thought he had an incurable disease. He said, "Laughter is inner jogging," in his book *The Healing Heart*.

Laughter brings oxygen into our bodies and creates a space where we have no worries. It releases the tension in our muscles. You can't feel stressed in the middle of a good laugh because your brain is focused on the physical act. It can't be worried about what to make for dinner at the same time.

Laughing is easy. Laughter is healing. And best of all, it's free! How can you create more laughter in your life?

> Laughter is healing and best of all, it's free.

One way is to be funny yourself. Izzy Gesell, a humorist in Northampton, Massachusetts, carries Groucho glasses with him in the car. At stop lights he puts them on and then slowly turns to look at the people in the car next to him. He says he gets all kinds of reactions, but eventually everyone, including Izzy, is laughing. The nice thing about people is that they are so unpredictable. You never know how they'll react to something you do. So ham it up and see how much laughing you can create for yourself and others.

Jokes are good, too, but only those that are not harmful or offensive. Laughter at someone else's expense is not soothing or healing. Laughter that comes out of sarcasm is not stress relieving. Think about it. You know it's true.

Find ways to laugh every day. Not much of a laugher,

you say? Here's a simple way to create some delight wherever you are.

Get a bottle of bubbles. Yes, bubbles. They cost about fifty cents. Keep them at work. Whenever the mood strikes you or when you notice that someone else could use a lift, blow bubbles over someone's partition. You will hear the sounds of surprise and delight within moments. Bubbles are happy and hard to ignore. Only the most hard-hearted person can withstand the loveliness and wonder of bubbles swirling in the air. For that person, get out the Groucho glasses!

Only one thing can be going on in your body at one time. Make it laughter for at least five minutes every day.

> "So, pack up your troubles in your old kit-bag
> And smile, smile, smile."
>
> ~George Asaf

The Fake Smile

So you don't want to laugh. You're not ready to laugh. You aren't willing to make the commitment to laugh. FINE! We'll start with something simple. I know you can smile, whatever your story or excuse may be. You'll probably tell me that you don't feel like smiling, that you don't have anything to smile about. So here's a five-second remedy for all of you veteran non-smilers.

You can feel better in five seconds by putting a fake smile on your face.

Paste a fake smile on your face. That's right, fake! You don't have to feel it, you don't have to care about it, you don't have to want it. Just put it there. I guarantee that within five seconds it will be real. Yes, it's true, the smile will be real. Do it right now. See? It works. Nobody seems to know why this works. Maybe it's because we feel so dorky with this stupid fake smile all over our faces and we can't help but laugh at ourselves. Whatever the reason, it does work and it works every single time. Not only will you have a real smile on your face, but having a real smile on your face cannot help but make you feel better. A fake smile that becomes real is funny. And so in giving ourselves the experience of smiling, we also give ourselves the experience of feeling lighter in an incredibly short time span.

The other thing to remember about smiling is that smiling is like laughing—it's contagious. If you smile more, the people around you will smile more too. And who knows, soon you might be willing to venture into the graduate school of laughter. Regardless of how you use it, you can feel better in five seconds simply by putting a fake smile on your face.

Do it again right now.

Feel better? Amazing, isn't it?

> *"To love oneself is the beginning of a lifetime romance."*
>
> ~Oscar Wilde

The Mirror Smile

This is not as ridiculous as it sounds. I want you to try something you may never have done before. I want you to look at yourself in the mirror. I mean, really look at yourself. Not while you are shaving or plucking your eyebrows or putting on make-up or brushing your teeth. Not while you are doing anything else other than looking at yourself. Bet you can't remember the last time you did this. That is, of course, if there ever was a last time. Maybe you've *never* looked at yourself in the mirror and just connected. Be excited, this is a great opportunity for you.

> Of all our relationships, the one we most often forget about is the one we have with ourselves.

Of all our relationships, the one we most often forget about is the one we have with ourselves. So go find a mirror, and just look at yourself. No, not at what's wrong with your face. You. Look at you. And say "Hello" and smile.

Feeling comfortable doing this may take some practice. That's fine. Practice.

What a lovely way to start the day. A deep, slow breath, a lovely smile, and "Good morning!" Creating a healthy relationship with yourself is the road to the good life.

You can start by simply looking in the mirror and seeing who's there.

"It is awfully hard work doing nothing."

~Oscar Wilde

quiet time

"Contemplation is the highest form of activity."

~Aristotle

Meditate

No, no, no. Don't skip this chapter. I know what you're saying, you've tried meditation, you can't do it, it takes too long, it's boring, you don't know how to do it right, and people who do it are weird. The truth is you can't do it wrong, and it only has to take as long as you want it to take. Although it is true that a lot of people who meditate are weird.

Meditation is one of the most ancient forms of relaxation—it's like taking a nap without going to sleep. In fact, it can be much more relaxing than sleep because your mind is busy while you sleep with all kinds of dreams. By emptying your mind, you give yourself a rest—meditation allows you to create a state of deep relaxation that is very healing to the entire body, your mind included. When the surface of a lake is still, you can see to the bottom very clearly. This is impossible when the surface is agitated by waves. In the same way, when the mind is still with no thoughts or desires, we experience peace and clarity.

The important thing to remember as you begin to meditate is not to give yourself a hard time if your mind wanders. It's not a problem; it's no big deal. Just bring your attention back to the meditation when you notice that your mind has wandered off to something else (as minds have been known to do).

Meditation is not as unusual as you think. In fact, many people are unknowingly in a state of meditation any number of times during a normal day. The key is to use meditation consciously as a "time out."

Read the following meditation into a tape recorder. One of the things we know is the voice we trust the most is our own.

Speak slowly in a calming tone. Allow your pace to get even slower in the middle portion of the meditation. Allow a few seconds for each ellipsis (…) in the text.

Five-Minute Relaxation Meditation

"Take a moment to find a comfortable position sitting or lying down and then close your eyes. Now, with your eyes closed, take a scan of your body to see if you are really comfortable. Notice if there are any places in your body that feel tight or stressed…and see if you can adjust your position so that your body is even more comfortable.

"Now, start to pay close attention to your breath. Feel the way your chest rises when you inhale…and feel how it falls when you exhale. Focus all of your attention on the simple inhale and exhale of your breath. As you do this, you will start to notice how your whole body begins to relax and calm down. With each breath you take, your body becomes more and more relaxed…and you notice that as your body becomes more and more relaxed, your breathing becomes slower…and as your breathing becomes slower, your body is more and more relaxed. Allow yourself to really enjoy this time of slowing down and relaxing. It can be so soothing and restful to give yourself some time to simply breathe deeply…relax…and rest.

"To allow yourself an even deeper relaxation, let your mind take you to a place that is beautiful and relaxing for you. Anyplace that feels relaxing to you. If you can't imagine a relaxing place that you have actually been to, create someplace new that you know would be peaceful. As you spend time in this relaxation paradise in your mind, allow yourself to completely take in the deep peacefulness and calm that you feel. Allow it to seep into your body and soul in a way that you will remember…in a way that will help you to remain calm and relaxed in other places in your life.

"Know that the feelings of relaxation that you experience here are always available to you…in any situation…at any time. These feelings are created and controlled by you…and you can recall these peaceful sensations anytime you want them. It is such a gift to be able to take just a few minutes to close your eyes and be in a relaxing, peaceful place…remember that you can return to this place anytime you desire by simply closing your eyes…focusing on your breathing…and recalling this experience.

"I'm going to give you some time to spend in silence so that you can deeply anchor yourself in this relaxing experience. It will only be a minute of real time…but just as you know that hours can seem to pass by in minutes when you are enjoying yourself, a minute can seem like an hour when you are deeply relaxed."

[Time one minute and then continue.]

"Begin to return your awareness to your body. Notice how your legs feel and the pressure of the seat or floor below you. Notice how your back feels against the surface. Slowly begin to move your fingers and hands and allow your mind and body to return to this room and this place. And when you are ready, allow your eyes to slowly open…and take a slow look around you at the amazing world that you inhabit!"

There are several meditation tapes and books. Play with them. Find a couple that you like and take a meditation break for five or ten minutes every day. Your body and your mind will thank you for it.

{ *"I believe in life after birth."*
~Maxie Dunham }

Breathe Well

The easiest no-nonsense way to take care of yourself quickly is to breathe deeply. When we're under stress, our muscles tense, and our breathing becomes shallow and rapid. One of the simplest ways to stop this stress response is to breathe deeply and slowly. It sounds simple, and it is. Most of us, however, do not breathe deeply under normal circumstances, so it may help to review the mechanics of deep breathing and how it helps us to relax.

Remember what I said about our ancestors? When prehistoric humans were in danger of attack, their muscles tensed and their breathing became rapid and shallow, as they prepared to run or fight. Their high level of tension was a means of preparing their bodies for optimum performance. Today, the causes of our stress are different, but our stress response is the same. However, since we're not running or fighting, our tension has no release and our stress response builds. One way to counteract the stress response is to learn how to breathe deeply and slowly—the *opposite* of how we breathe when under stress.

Here's something we've been doing since the moment we were born and most of us do it wrong. Now you're saying to yourself, "I must not be doing it totally wrong because I'm alive." And granted, if you're reading this book, you probably are alive. You must be breathing at some level, but I'm talking about breathing that does more than simply keep us alive.

Deep breathing is not always natural to adults. Watch the way a baby breathes; the area beneath the chest goes in and out. Most adults breathe from the chest. This is shallower breathing, so less oxygen is taken in with each breath. As a result, the blood is forced to move through the system quickly so enough oxygen gets to the brain and organs. Higher blood pressure results.

Take a moment and notice how you breathe. What's moving? How fast are your breaths? How deep are they? The correct way to breathe is far different than the way most of us do it. Doing it the right way, however, is amazingly easy.

Put your hand on your belly. Now take a deep breath in through your nose. You want to feel the air filling your body starting down at your belly, up through your diaphragm, and into your chest—much like filling a glass with water. When you exhale, you empty the glass. Try counting to five as you inhale and think the word "in," then count to five as you exhale and think the word "out." Work up to being able to count up to ten for each inhale and each exhale.

> Every breath you take should start and end in your belly.

Every breath you take should start in your belly and end in the same place. American fashion is not big on bellies. No one is supposed to have one and even if you do, it certainly shouldn't be moving around. But breathing completely and correctly creates enough benefit to fly in the face of fashion. Breathing fully may require practice.

One of my clients believes the most valuable thing I taught him was how to breathe well. He insists it has saved his career any number of times in any number of stupid meetings. He does at least five complete deep breaths before he speaks and says that by the time he's done, he's less bothered by what's happening around him. Before deep breathing, he yelled a lot.

It upset him and didn't do much for those in the vicinity either. He also rarely got his way—big surprise. (For those of you who actually are surprised, email me and I'll explain why he didn't get his way and why people who yell often don't). Now he almost always gets what he wants and he's relaxed as he goes about it.

In addition to normal deep breathing for everyday wellness, there are a number of special breathing techniques to use in highly stressful situations. Some can be done right where you are, in the situation. Some may require that you find a space by yourself for a few minutes.

There are thousands of breathing techniques you could use and, like meditation, there are books and tapes galore. For now, I'm going to share three techniques that you can use to calm yourself down quickly.

Relaxed and Calm

Inhale and exhale through your nose, keeping your mouth closed.

As you inhale, turn your head to the right and think "relaxed." Then as you exhale, turn your head to the left and think "calm." Make your breathing deep and do the exercise slowly. It's a nice stretch for your neck, too. Start this exercise with a goal of three minutes and work your way up to eleven minutes.

Belly Bounce

In this Kundalini yoga technique, the inhale and exhale are also through your nose with your mouth closed.

The inhale is actually four short inhales, almost like sniffing. Your belly should bounce. The exhale is a single long breath.

This is a good technique to use if you are feeling depressed or tired. Three minutes is usually plenty.

Weil's Relaxing Breath

Andrew Weil has an excellent breathing technique for relaxation in his book *Eight Weeks to Optimum Health*. He calls it "Relaxing Breath."

Place your tongue on the roof of your mouth just behind your front teeth, and keep it there throughout.

Exhale completely making an audible sound; Weil recommends a *whoosh*. Close your mouth and inhale through your nose to a count of four. Hold your breath for a count of seven and then exhale audibly through your mouth (keep your tongue behind your teeth) for a count of eight. Repeat four times.

This technique will take some practice, but it is very effective. Try it before going to bed at night. Weil likes to use it if he wakes up in the middle of the night. I like to use it just before I go to sleep.

> "Writing is easy. All you do is stare at a blank sheet of paper until drops of blood form on your forehead."
> —Gene Fowler

Write

I am a person who resisted keeping a journal for decades. I think of a journal as some cumbersome, intellectual thing. The people I know who keep a journal write for hours every day and go to classes and workshops and read books about it. This kind of commitment to a spiral-bound notebook was always much more than I was willing to make. So I smiled politely when people waxed poetic about their journaling experiences.

Because I am also a person who resists what everyone else is doing, I only recently read the book *Simple Abundance* by Sarah Ban Breathnach. And while her name is a mouthful, the book is wonderful. I found her ideas about journals to be quite different than anything I've ever heard before. It gave me permission to keep a journal in my own way and my own time.

> Put everything you've always wanted to say on paper.

Think about a journal as a way of talking to yourself. You aren't recording something that will be published (I don't think) or that will be read by other people. (My friend Carolyn Tertes has an agreement with her sons that they will destroy her journal unread the instant she dies.) It doesn't have to be grammatically correct or pretty. It's just a way to get whatever is stuck in your head and distracting you out on paper and out of your way.

Don't be surprised if your first attempts are all whining. Give yourself permission to write whatever you think or feel. For the first couple of months, don't go back and reread anything you have written. This is not writing for the press or the public or a grade—this is moving stuff out of your head and heart and onto a piece of paper so you can have more space in your life for the things happening at the moment.

Writing is a great thing that can be done anywhere, at any time, dressed in any way. Write on anything. Write whenever the mood strikes you. Write a single paragraph, write twenty pages. Do it in bed in the morning, at your desk, sitting in the car waiting for the drive-up teller, curled up in the most comfortable chair in the house.

If the idea of a journal still seems daunting, write letters, memos, or notes. To anyone, to everyone, to no one. Just don't send them unless you are writing them with the intention of sending them. Writing a letter to someone focuses our attention on what it is we're wanting to say to that person. So say it in writing, but know that the best mailbox is often a bottom dresser drawer.

I encourage my clients to write thrillingly hateful memos and then put them somewhere safe out of the office (we don't want them sent to anyone by mistake!) Two days later, rewrite them. The issues are somewhere in there and the spite, having been splattered all over the memo in the heat of the moment, is no longer necessary.

Take everything you've always wanted to say and put it on paper. It's incredibly soothing.

> *"There must be quite a few things a hot bath won't cure, but I don't know many of them."*
> ~Sylvia Plath

Take a Bath

Water. Plain, everyday tap water. Heat it and suddenly you have the makings of a luxurious, restful experience. I know people who have bought houses because of the size of the bathtub. What is it about water? Maybe it's that we start our lives in fluid. For nine months, we're surrounded by warm, nurturing waves. I believe one of the appeals of the ocean is that the ebb and tide is reminiscent of the womb. What could be more relaxing or feel safer than going back to the place where someone else took care of absolutely everything?

There are lots of ways to do water, both actively and passively. You can run through the sprinkler, swim in a pool, find one of those water slide places and go completely nuts, canoe down a quiet river, race down a rapids, stand under a waterfall, or walk in the rain (sing in the rain at the same time and that would take care of a couple of things!)

Still, at the end of the day, or the end of the week, the cheapest way I know to treat yourself well is to turn off the phone, turn down the lights, and get into a tub of hot water. Can't you hear yourself sighing as you slide down into it? Doesn't everything else go away? You can do it fancy and add candles, scented oil, nibbles, a book, music, a partner, or any combination thereof. You can do it spare. Just get the water to the perfect temperature and treat yourself to time without any of the clothing we wear for the world—physical, mental, or emotional.

Bathing is about being. A shower is great—it gets you clean. But a bath is a whole different thing. It's spiritual. And maybe that's because we all start out floating in water and it's a thing that connects us to each other regardless of the multitude of differences we conjure up almost as soon as we leave that sacred water.

I'm starting to sound meta-physical.

Get in the bathtub and see what you think. And don't say you don't have time. You have to be clean anyway. Besides, you can't eat in the shower.

A bath is a whole different thing. It's spiritual.

"*People who make no noise are dangerous.*"

~Jean de la Fontaine

noisy time

Groan

Groaning is simply sighing with an attitude. You've had the experience of little bits of groaning in your life. Now what you want to do is allow yourself to groan fully, passionately, and with energy.

Take a long, slow, deep belly breath in through your nose and then let all of the air come out through your mouth with an audible sound. Groan for all you're worth. Do it about five times and you'll find your shoulders are two inches lower than before.

It's great to groan by yourself...and it's better to groan in a group! Group groaning is particularly satisfying and can become addictive.

Groaning is excellent pre-work for my favorite advanced breathing technique, screaming.

{ *"More energy! More energy!"*

~Napoleon Bonaparte }

Scream

Have you ever *really* screamed? Full out, no stops? Screaming requires us to take in vast quantities of oxygen, so naturally when we're finished we feel much more relaxed. Your screaming will get better as your breathing improves because the more air you can take in, the longer, louder, and more blood-curdling your screams will be.

Screaming is wonderfully satisfying which may be because it's essentially a forbidden activity. In this land of courteous, polite, and genteel behavior, screaming is an unconventional and wonderfully, delightfully inappropriate stress reliever. It works great. And fast. Which is why it's so much fun.

It's a fairly innocuous way to take a walk on the wild side. Instead of saying, "Couldn't you just scream," do it.

Screaming does require some preparation. This is not something that you want to be doing in the bank or at the post office. Screaming in the car is good, but not while you're driving and probably not while anyone else is driving either. Screaming in the house is good if all the windows are down and you've warned anyone else who happens to be home. You might want to invite them to join you!

> Instead of saying "Couldn't you just scream," do it.

If you feel a need to ease into screaming, you can always scream into a pillow. It's not as effective, but it's not bad.

As to the scream itself, it's important that you take the deepest possible belly breath and that you scream from your diaphragm, which is just above your belly. If you scream from your throat, you're going ...lf and then you won't be able to scream o good screams is usually all it takes. Thre ber. But don't limit yourself—if it feel not done, just keep on screaming.

because I'm ...

> *"Let us make a joyful noise..."*
> ~The Bible

Sing

Everybody sings. Yes, everybody, even you. Whoever told you that you couldn't sing was wrong.

Everybody sings. It's our heritage as human beings. We have always had song as part of our culture, no matter where, no matter when. People have been singing and chanting since the beginning of time.

Singing feels good. It's an easy, less mindful way to do breath work. While I don't mind breathing exercises at all and they work really well, I'd rather turn on Bob Seger's "Old Time Rock 'N' Roll" at full blast and sing along. By the end of the song, I feel great and I don't even know I've been doing breath work.

I'm not a great singer—no one is going to pay money to hear me sing. So I sing whenever I'm in the ⸯr, often when I'm in the shower, and even more when lone in the house. The car is my favorite though, ⸯ can have the music wrapped around me using

34

far fewer decibels than it takes to get the same effect in the house. Besides, I like to bounce around in the car, keeping time on the steering wheel.

I think other people who do this look like morons, I scoff at them as I drive by. But I just know that when I do it, I look incredibly cool and that everyone driving by envies and admires me. Assume that you'll look cool, too.

If singing in the car is too intimidating, then start by singing in the shower. No one can be graded while singing in the shower. It's not allowed. All shower singing is acceptable, but if you're worried about it, get one of those shower radios, turn it up, and sing along. That way, no one can hear you at all and you get to sing.

The late, great choir director of our church always said, "Singing is like praying twice." What could be bad about that?

> *"What happens to all the tears we do not shed?"*
> ~Jules Renard

Cry

Has it been a long time since you had a good cry? I mean an all out, sobbing, blubbering, nose-running cry? Do you think something catastrophic has to happen before you're allowed to let yourself go and cry? Au contraire, mon ami.

My friend Steven only cries at funerals. Sometimes he hardly knows the person who died. When we were at one of those funerals I asked him what was up. His crying seemed inappropriate for the particular occasion. He didn't know the person at all. We were business acquaintances of the spouse. He thought about it for awhile and said he thought that it was a place where crying was socially acceptable and he could, therefore, do a lot of useful crying about a lot of things while he was there. He also said that he thought he had good access to his feelings at a funeral and it made sense to him to go for it. I thought that it made sense too, but I also thought it was sad that he has to store it up until he has the opportunity to go to a funeral.

Crying is cleansing. It removes pollutants from the body. According to a study cited by Robert Ornstein and David Sobel in *The Healing Brain*, analysis of human tears emitted because of pain or joy show a different chemical make-up than tears emitted because of eye irritations caused by getting something in your eye or cutting up an onion. "Real" tears contain higher levels of toxic substances that the body is evidently eliminating through crying. That's good news— one more way to get rid of the "junk" we accumulate. Think of it as cleaning out your closet or, even better, taking out the trash. (None of us cleans our closets often enough for that to be a useful metaphor. A good cry once a week is what we're after, not once a year.)

> Crying removes pollutants from the body.

Another interesting factoid cited by Paul P. Pearsall in *Superimmunity* is that deep and prolonged crying in men has been found to normalize testosterone levels. High testosterone levels play a role in aggressive and competitive behavior and have been shown to be connected to strokes and heart attacks. I'd much rather men were crying than hitting. And I have to believe that they would think it was better too, if they tried it.

And, get this, 80 percent of people studied reported that they feel better after crying. That number was cited in *Psychology Today*. 80 percent! This is definitely something to get in on!

I come from a family that doesn't "show" what are considered unpleasant emotions. No, I'm not blaming my parents for anything; they're quite terrific. I did, however, have to relearn how to cry when I was an adult. It took me awhile to do it, but it's a skill I'm very glad to have. I cry at the movies, I cry during songs, I cry at church, I cry when everything is wonderful, I cry when everything isn't. And I do feel lots better afterwards. You can, too.

If crying isn't something you do naturally or if it embarrasses you for any reason, it's okay to be a closet crier until you get the hang of it. Start by noticing what brings up "teary" feelings for you. A particular song, a movie, a person. Then use whatever it is to "create" a good cry. Do this when you're completely alone or with someone you trust. Crying alone can feel very isolating. Crying with someone you trust who keeps his or her mouth shut and just lets you cry can be incredibly liberating. If you aren't ready to do it with anyone around, keep reminding yourself that this is a good thing to do, a healthy thing to do. Because it's true. Crying is normal and natural. It's not shameful or weak. If you find that you simply cannot cry, don't give yourself a hard time. That's the opposite of what this book is about. Instead, talk with a friend about your experiences with crying or not crying. If even that's too much, try writing about it for yourself. When we've lost a natural function that serves a purpose, it's important to begin to find ways to bring it back into our lives.

Crying is a very useful stress reducer and it's good for you. You don't have to wait for a funeral.

"I am a restlessness
inside a stillness
inside a restlessness."

~Dodie Smith

move
around

Exercise

This isn't about health clubs, fitness centers, leotards, spandex, or weights, unless you want it to be. You already know how many times a week you're supposed to exercise and for how long, so we're going to skip all that. Instead, I want to suggest a number of easy exercises that you can do sitting at your desk, in the car, standing in line at the supermarket, or wherever you happen to be.

The other thing I want you to do is simply to start moving more. One of the simplest ways to get more exercise is to take the stairs. If you work in a building with more than one floor and you've been using the elevator, STOP! You can start small and only use the stairs when going one flight, but once you can do that easily, add another. This is a tremendous way to increase your stamina and your energy level and you'll wind up with better-looking legs, too.

Another simple fitness secret, and I know that this will be tremendously controversial, is to put down the remote. Going back to those dark days of having to stand up and walk over to change the channel is good for your body and good for your mind.

Try parking the car four spaces further than you normally would. When you're feeling particularly ambitious, park at the end of the lot. Every little bit counts.

The exercises coming up are to relieve tension in your head, neck, and shoulders—the "stress triangle"—where so many of us hold much of our tension. None of them should take more than two minutes.

Remember—you can do these anywhere and any time, dressed in anything. Learning how to release the tension in these muscles can help us relax and "de-stress."

To find your "stress triangle," place your left hand on your right shoulder. Move your fingers halfway in toward your neck. You're at one point of the triangle. The second point is the same place off your left shoulder. The third point is on your forehead, between your eyes. This is the "stress triangle."

Our muscles tighten to prepare us for that old fight or flight response to danger. But usually, we don't need that kind of protection. When our muscles shorten, and then hold that position, metabolites (the waste products from muscle activity) get trapped, causing pain. The pain is released when the muscle regains its natural length.

The following simple stretches and rolls can help relieve tightness in your "stress triangle."

Neck roll

Stretch your right ear to your right shoulder, keeping your left shoulder pulled down. Roll your head down so your chin is on your chest. Continue on to your left side. Do rolls from side to side. Begin with eight and build up to sixteen. Be sure to use deep breathing when you do all the stretches. Deep breathing will make all the exercises more effective. It's also tough to relax when you're holding your breath. Try it and see.

Shoulder shrug
Draw a big circle with your shoulders, one at a time. Start with four, build up to eight times, going forward, then back.

Pick fruit
With one hand, reach up as if you were picking an apple from a tree slightly ahead and far above you. Go from one arm to the other, building up to eight times on each side.

Massage yourself
Use your right hand to work on your left shoulder and left hand on your right shoulder. Work your fingers gently but firmly, beginning with your shoulder blade, moving up toward the neck and including the scalp.

Standing body roll
Let your head roll forward until your chin is on your chest. Keep rolling down as your knees begin to bend. When your hands are hanging near your knees, rest there a moment and slowly roll back up. Work up to ten times.

> *"Yoga is the ability to direct the mind exclusively towards an object and sustain that direction without any distractions."*
> ~Patanjali

Yoga

The word "yoga" is Sanskrit and means "union." Serious practitioners believe that the practice of yoga joins the individual soul with the Supreme Spirit. For the rest of us, yoga is a set of physical movements or exercises that creates flexibility of body and peace of mind.

There are zillions of books, tapes, and videos for all levels of practice and many different forms of yoga. I happen to prefer Kundalini yoga which has a lot of breath work in it. Most people in America practice Hatha yoga which also is very good.

Yoga is not something you would normally do for five or ten minutes. However, there are many single postures that can easily be done in a minute or two almost anywhere. Below are five yoga postures you can try. The first three are Kundalini which combines breath with movement and the others are Hatha which is about holding a posture and gaining flexibility.

"Elvis Pelvis"

That's the affectionate name for this Kundalini yoga posture from my friend Kenny. You simply roll your hips around in a circle while keeping your feet, your knees, and your shoulders forward and your hands on your hips. Do eighteen in one direction and then eighteen in the other. You probably want to be in a closed office or other fairly private space when you do these. Or maybe you don't.

Kundalini Hip Roll

This is a really good, simple yoga posture for the lower back. It takes very little time and will keep your lower back flexible and strong. I also use it immediately if I feel a strain in my back.

Sit on the floor with your legs crossed. Place your hands lightly on your knees. Roll your hips forward. Your back will arch. Now roll your hips back. Your back will bow. Inhale through your nose when you roll forward, exhale as you roll back. Begin doing this posture for one minute and work your way up to three. Be careful not to pull yourself forward with your hands; your hips create the motion.

The Mountain

This Hatha yoga posture is deceptively simple. It will get you grounded in a minute, and you'll feel refreshed afterward.

Stand very straight, with your feet together and your spine straight. Gently engage the muscles of your feet, legs, buttocks, and abdomen, but make sure your shoulders are relaxed. When you feel very grounded, raise your arms over your head and interlock your fingers with just your index fingers pointing upward. Stretch tall without tensing your shoulders. On an exhale, bring your arms back to your sides and relax.

The Half Moon

The Half Moon gives you a terrific side stretch, building flexibility and strength at the same time.

Stand in the Mountain pose, with your hands over your head, fingers interlocked, with your index fingers pointing upward. Now stretch to the right, pushing your left hip to the left and stretching your hands and arms to the right. Feel the stretch all along the left side of your body. Count three breaths in this position, then on an inhale, stand up straight, and on the exhale, stretch to the other side. Count three breaths while you stretch along the right side of your body. Come up straight on an inhale, then lower your arms on the exhale. Stand quietly for a moment.

Cat and Cow

These two stretches done together give your spine a little workout and strengthen the muscles in your back and abdomen.

Get down on the floor on your hands and knees, with your back flat like a table top. On an inhale, arch your back and look up. Pull your shoulder blades together, and be careful not to strain your lower back. On an exhale, round your back and look down, pulling your abdomen in and stretching your spine. Inhale and arch, exhale and round. Repeat about five times, then sit back on your heels and rest for three breaths.

Yoga is incredibly relaxing. It's a wonderful thing to do after work. It's good for your body, your mind, and your soul. You can do it in a class or by yourself at home.

If you hate to exercise, yoga is for you. You will get a good workout and not be winded or sweaty. There is some discomfort in the beginning as you stretch things that haven't been stretched in a long time, but it goes away quickly and it's worth it. One of the nice things about yoga is that you get better at it very quickly. My friend Mary-Jane and I travel together every year in March. We're usually gone for about ten days. We do yoga each morning and every year we are amazed at how much more flexible we are on the last morning. In just ten days we see real results.

"Bodies never lie."
~Agnes De Mille

Dance

I bet you've got your hands covering your eyes, as you shake your head saying, "No, no, no, no, no." You thought that giving singing a try was really going out on a limb, but dancing, DANCING, for goodness sake, is out of the question. (And then there are the seven of you who are jumping up and down because you love to dance and you know it's good for you and now you have permission to do it more.)

Dancing is inherent to us, just as singing is. Human beings have been dancing since they stood upright. In fact, it's probably why they stood upright. It's hard to dance on all fours, particularly in pairs or groups. A circle dance on all fours would represent a major challenge. Anyway, I digress.

Dancing is joyful. It not only gives our minds a rest, it gives our bodies the opportunity to move. You may find pumping iron a joy or feel great spending forty-five minutes on the Stairmaster, but I submit that the joy to be found in dancing is different. It is a joy that bubbles up from the marrow of our bones and connects us as humans. Watch the faces of people who are not afraid to dance. There is a light that shines from them that I don't believe you will ever see in a fitness center or at a road race. As dancers sweat, they smile. And their smiles are radiant.

Dancing is a gift you give yourself.

I'm not talking about professional dancers. I'm talking about the folks down at the K of C hall at the corner doing country western dance and the people at the Town Hall doing the rumba and the couples downtown at the clubs moving freely around the floor.

There are lots of ways to bring dance into your life. Pull the curtains, put on the music, and move. Close your eyes if you want to.

Pick a kind of dance you'd like to do and go find lessons. There is dancing going on everywhere. If you feel bashful, country western line dancing may be a good place to start. You don't have to have a partner, most of the dances are easy to learn, the music makes you want to move, and you get to dance (and lose yourself, if necessary) in a big crowd. I've also noticed that country western dancers are particularly nice, very forgiving, and extremely willing to help out a new dancer. I've stood next to people who talked me through an entire dance and never blinked an eye. I've done couple dances where the pair in front of us gave helpful hints as we moved through the dance. This isn't something you'll find as much with ballroom, but it's also true of folk dancing which is another kind of dance where you usually don't need a partner.

You can dance with someone else or you can dance alone. You can dance in the living room for five minutes or go out on the town for the evening.

Dancing is a gift you give yourself. Try it.

"What do you want to be?"
"I would like to be myself.
I tried to be other things
but I always failed."

~Anonymous

kindergarten
magic

"People say that life is the thing,
but I prefer reading."

–Logan Pearsall

Read Aloud

One of the things you may notice about this book is that a lot of the chapters involve activities that you probably haven't done in a while. There's a good reason for that. Many of the things that work quickly and are tremendously relaxing are things that we did when we were younger, much, much younger. I don't know what Great Decider there is in each of us that lets us know when to put these "childish" things away, but we all have one. And sure enough, the very things that are good for all of us and work quickly are the very things that we give up to be "adult." Like there's something so terrific about being an adult it's worth not playing with Tinkertoys anymore. Get out the Tinkertoys and see if you think it was worth it. I keep mine right at hand now that I've rediscovered them. If you don't think they're better than the evening news, send me a note.

Reading aloud falls into this "gave it up to be a big person" category. When was the last time someone read you a story? Not out of the newspaper or a magazine, but a "story" story. It's a completely decadent, rich experience to have someone read aloud to you. It's luscious. And no matter how much you like to read yourself, it's totally different when someone else is doing it.

This is a pastime that will not last five or ten minutes for long. You can do it for short periods of time. You can work it out with someone else to read a book together out loud, one chapter at a time, each of you taking turns, but I guarantee you will soon be spending more than ten minutes at it. It's too wonderful an experience to stop that soon.

This is one of those good "Hey, let's do this instead of watching TV" things. Try it with children—of any age—and watch how your time together changes.

When my son was thirteen, we spent a hurricane weekend in New York in a fancy condo. The man who was our host had just gotten a Garrison Keillor book of stories and I remember sitting curled up in a big over-stuffed sofa reading that book aloud. What an incredible way to spend a rainy afternoon. We were mesmerized, totally relaxed, and happy.

Want to know how to start? Go get a bunch of children's books. *Where The Wild Things Are*, *Old Turtle*, *The Polar Express*, *Horton Hatches An Egg*, *Bartholomew Cubbins and the Oobleck*, and *Madeline*. And then prepare yourself for a sinfully pleasurable experience.

> *"The highest condition of art is artlessness."*
>
> ~Henry David Thoreau

Color and Cut

Remember coloring books? Remember blocks? Remember clay? Boy, weren't they the best.

I assume if you haven't laughed much lately that you probably haven't colored much lately either. You won't believe how good it is until you try it. I'm not talking about becoming Wyatt or Picasso. I'm talking about putting crayon to paper and just being with it.

Ten minutes with a box of Crayolas is a great rest. It soothes the savage beast and calms the ravaged mind. (The box of twenty-four Crayolas has all the good colors but if you're feeling adventurous, the box of sixty-four has the exotic ones.)

You can use blank paper or a coloring book, whichever feels good to you. You can keep your crayons and paper or book in your desk or in your briefcase.

I know that life in a lot of households would be infinitely improved if those train and bus commuters colored on the way home rather than reading the bad news in newspapers or talking on one of those abominable cell phones.

If you have to start as a closet colorer, I understand. Lock the door, pull the blinds, and go to it. It's absolute bliss.

I know this not only because I do it, but because I have included it as a part of my stress reduction workshops. It's the part of the workshop that no one wants to end. (I've found that I have to give the group a warning

> **Ten minutes with a box of Crayolas is a great rest.**

about eight minutes before it's time to stop or I have the possibility of revolution on my hands—which is not stress reducing.)

If you're very adventurous, you can use crayons and colored paper and scissors and glue. Make things or make collages or just cut up a bunch of stuff and stick it all together.

If you want to feel better, color instead of watching television some evening. You're not going to believe the difference.

"The best kind of conversation is that which may be called thinking aloud."

~William Hazlitt

talk

With Someone Else

This isn't exactly talking as you know it. This is a special kind of talking. This is talking where someone is actually seriously listening to you. To be able to talk like this requires a friend or colleague who's willing to play the part of the listener. Finding someone like that and creating an agreement with her or him will be the hardest part of the exercise.

I think people used to be better listeners. Maybe it's because it wasn't considered polite in days of yore to tell everyone what you thought about what they were saying.

What I notice now is that people are so busy being "helpful," they don't have time to listen to what is being said or to consider whether anyone really wants their help or not.

In my own experience, I've found that people like to figure things out for themselves, even when they've asked for help or advice. I have a good friend who is always asking for advice and then telling the advisor why the advice is wrong. Conversations with her used to be very tedious and frustrating. Now I just don't play and we're fine. She'll ask me what I think, I ask her what she thinks. Eventually, she decides for herself or goes off to ask someone else. Either way, I don't get caught trying to think for someone else. No matter how well you know someone, no matter what the situation, the truth is you haven't had that person's life experience to date and so your answer doesn't really apply. Save your energy and just listen to them instead.

So, ask someone to listen to you. Just listen, no helpful comments, no advice, no stories about when the same thing happened to them. You may have to be patient as your listener learns how to listen. Just keep reminding them if they interrupt you or start speaking at the end of your sentences that you just want them to listen, that's all.

Set a time limit. Start with five minutes. You can work your way up to an hour if you'd like, but start slow.

It's a good idea to have this listening and speaking be reciprocal. You may not switch roles every time one of you wants to be listened to, but if you want someone to become a good listener for you, it probably stands to reason that they would be more willing if they knew that they were going to get a turn, too.

Knowing someone will just listen gives us tremendous freedom to talk about what's important to us and to hear ourselves as we think something through. It's very different than thinking about something in your head or trying to talk about something when you know the other person can and will speak at any time while you are trying to speak.

Get yourself heard. It's a big relief. And you'll learn a lot about yourself and what's going on with you.

> *"Words make another place, a place to escape to your spirit alone."*
> ~Robert MacNeil

With Yourself

Let's go back to the mirror. When you first looked at yourself in the mirror, what popped into your mind? I know that when I first looked what popped into my mind wasn't positive.

I believe that the most negative things we hear about ourselves are mostly things we ourselves think. When I hear people making deprecating remarks about themselves, I wonder what they must be thinking about themselves if they are willing to say such awful things out loud.

I'm big on surrounding myself with positive thoughts. I hope that they'll seep in and start to overshadow the negative "I'm not good enough" junk that always seems to be floating around in my head. I have lots of sayings on the refrigerator and lots stuck up all around my office. Things like, "Count your blessings," and "When one door closes, another one opens," and, "Most people are about as happy as they make their minds up to be." I used to have very sarcastic, witty sayings all around, but at some point I realized I could do all that put-down talk very nicely by myself and I didn't need a lot of reminders around me all day and all night. In one of my offices when I was a junior executive I had a parody of the 23rd Psalm that said, "Yea, though I walk through the valley of the shadow of death I will fear no evil for I am the meanest son of a bitch in the valley." I thought it was very cute. Now I have the 23rd Psalm in its entirety close at hand wherever I am and I recite it all the time. Because now I understand that what I want to embed in my mind is, "surely goodness and mercy will follow me all the days of my life." Maybe it's just part of my growing up, but I like "soft" sayings much more.

> The most negative things we hear about ourselves are mostly things we ourselves think.

Find a single sentence or phrase that is true about you or that you want to be true about you and whenever you "hear" something about yourself in your head that you don't like simply replace it with your new phrase. Something as simple as, "I am a good person doing good things," or "I'm the best." Or think exactly the opposite of the negative thought.

There are many books and tapes with affirmations (that's the technical term for these positive statements I'm talking about. There's a technical term for everything today, isn't there?) I think you can easily come up with a bunch for yourself, but if you want ideas or someone to say them along with you, go to the bookstore or library and knock yourself out.

> "To believe in God is impossible—
> not to believe in Him is absurd."
>
> ~Voltaire

Prayer

This will be short and sweet. God either is or isn't. If God is, then regular prayer makes sense. We talk to the Creator and the Creator listens. Sometimes we get what we want, sometimes we don't. If God is, then he/she/it knows best and if we don't get what we want it's because the Creator knows best. That's cool.

If God isn't, then we talk to the Creator and no one is listening. Sometimes we get what we want and sometimes we don't. If God isn't, then it's just that sometimes we don't get what we want. And that's cool, too. Do you really expect to always get what you want?

In the meantime, people who pray regularly seem to be calmer, happier, healthier, and more grateful for what they do have. Not bad.

So if God is, great. If God isn't, prayer still appears to have a lot of benefit.

Okay? Works for me. End of chapter.

"Let even a fountain
have a rest."

~Alexei Konstantinovich Tolstoi

escape

"It is better to have loafed and lost than never to have loafed at all."

~James Thurber

Waste Time

Let's talk about this time thing for a minute. Does anyone really know what time it is? What is time anyway? We operate as if we know, but the truth is clock time is made up. Time as we know it is completely artificial what with time zones and daylight savings time. Who are we kidding?

Time is something we use to beat ourselves up. We're always "racing against the clock," trying to find "just five more minutes," "running out of time," "making time" to do things, or making up "lost time." Basically, we're driving ourselves insane.

Remember once more the 1950s when they told us that technology was going to create a world where we'd have more leisure time than work time. The problem was going to be finding enough leisure time activities to keep ourselves active and alert. Work was going to take up a very small percentage of our time and boredom was going to be our biggest concern.

They sure hit that one right on the head, didn't they? Instead none of us have any time for anything anymore. We're in a mad race to get the work done, get the kids wherever they're going, get dinner made, read what we didn't get to at work, rush to work out, rush to relax, and all the time we're watching the clock—like it's going to help us solve something.

Here's a big "Aha"—there isn't going to be enough time to do everything ever again. Technology has made us slaves, not liberated us. We can't get away from the means to do more and more for longer and longer.

Stop watching the clock.

So stop watching the clock. Take a deep breath (and now that you've read the chapter on breathing, you can do it the right way. Is that exciting or what?), close your eyes, and waste some time. Take a snooze, go for a walk, read a trashy book, see a silly movie. Everything will be waiting for you when you resurface. I promise.

You've got all the time in the world.

> *"Nature is whole and yet never finished."*
> ~Goethe

Go Outside

I try not to make too many assumptions. I find them deadly. However, I am assuming that if you're reading this book, you spend less time outdoors than other people. I doubt that many people who work outside or who are very active physically involving the outdoors would have use for this book. I may be wrong. If I am, let me know.

Most of us work indoors in recycled air and fluorescent light. Did you know that fluorescent lights blink and that your eyes have to adjust that blinking out? When I worked for a large corporation, I found that the only way for me to be effective after 3 o'clock in the afternoon was to have the fluorescent lights that were over my head disconnected. I was fortunate to have work spaces where I could do that and access to the people who could do it for me. Until I figured out what was going on, I simply faded by 3 p.m. It felt like my brain was fried. I was lucky to work at a suburban location in a "campus" environment. When I felt completely depleted, it was easy to walk outside and breathe some fresh air. If the weather was nice, I might walk for ten minutes. If not, I would just stand under the portico and breathe and look at the land, the trees, the plants, the birds.

Nature has a cadence far different than the one technology has created for most of us. While a wild storm may whip through occasionally, nature is mostly relaxed. Things grow over time. Snow falls softly. Waves roll in. Sunrises and sunsets are not hurried.

We are awed by the majesty and grandeur of a big storm because it is unusual, the tempo is different from the norm.

Being outside allows us to fall into rhythm with nature and because her rhythm is relaxed, our rhythm relaxes, too. People who are outside for the pleasure of being there are rarely harried. Watch people in a park, at the beach, hiking a trail. There is a different energy even if they are doing something that moves quickly.

Give yourself the gift of several small forays outside each day. Maybe it will only be for two or three minutes. Just get out there and take some deep breaths. It works as well in Manhattan as it does in Wyoming. If you go out for lunch, look around you. Deepen your breathing, look at the sky, notice the flowers or the trees or the snow.

Go outside each day to see the wonder of the earth and feel your connection to the whole world. You'll come back into your work space with a different attitude.

> *"It is in his pleasure that a man really lives; it is from his leisure that he constructs the true fabric of self."*
>
> ~Agnes Repplier

Go Home

Here's a novel idea. Even if they are paying you tremendous amounts of overtime or one of those incredibly inflated salaries, you owe it to yourself to leave work on time at least two or three days a week. Money does not replace time. Nor does it replace the wear and tear on your body, mind, and soul.

I can't tell you how many corporate executives I've worked with who insisted that nothing in their lives was more important than their families. They didn't seem to notice that their families were the people that they didn't see. The people that they did most of their complaining about (who shall remain nameless) were the people they spent all of their time with. Does this make sense to you? It never did to me.

There is probably nothing I can think of that has garnered me more thanks and gratitude than when I have worked with people and insisted that they leave work on time at least three days a week. I get thank you notes from spouses. I get praise from the clients. It's like I've given them their lives back. And in a way I have. Of course, what I've done is pretty simple and they could have done it for themselves years before I came on the scene. But they haven't. Instead, they pay me money to tell them to go home. So I tell them, they go home, and they're happy.

So, go ahead. Shock everyone. Go home.

> "Remember wherever you go,
> there you are."
> –Earl MacRaucht

Go Away

In this world of technology, nothing has been more adversely influenced than vacations. I know of almost no one, including me, who goes away for a vacation and is really totally away. Even I feel that I have to check my voice mail twice a day when I'm away. And having written that I just decided that I'm not going to do it anymore.

The word vacation comes from the Latin word "vacatio." It means "freedom." Vacation is defined as "a time of respite from something; a scheduled period during which activity is suspended." Does anyone do that anymore? Well, as of this moment I'm going to. There's no reason not to. Who can't live without me for a week or two? Get serious. Everyone can. And everyone can live without you, too. If you think they can't, forgive me, but you're wrong.

I'm not talking about not telling your kids where you're going to be and not checking in on them or not giving your mother the phone number where you can be reached in case of an emergency (you better give your mother the number or you'll have real stress when you get back). I'm talking about the people you work for and work with. They can manage without you while you get some much deserved time off.

Once upon a time, I worked for a big insurance company. I had a job I truly loved and a boss who was terrific, but he thought people should call in twice a day while they were away on vacation because he liked to do that himself. The people who worked with and for me wanted me to call in twice a day "just in case." Along with this job I loved, I also had a ten-year-old son. I thought pretty highly of him, too. And I believed that when he and I were away on vacation together, he deserved to have my time and my attention in the same way my colleagues had it when I was at work.

So I talked with my boss and I talked with the people with whom I worked. Here is what I told them: "If something comes up that you would normally talk with me about and you're not sure what to do, just do what you would do if I didn't exist." Think how empowering that is. The people who worked with me were intelligent adults. They didn't need me to tell them what to do day-to-day and they didn't need me to tell them what to do in a crisis either. They just liked to have me around to bounce stuff off of. But require me? No way. No one is indispensable, thank goodness! People leave, people die, people lose interest, people move on. And because of those things, you can go on vacation and be absent for a week. Take two. With today's stress levels it takes the first four days of a vacation just to begin to relax. Whatever is going on at work will be there when you get back.

Look carefully at the word "vacation." See the "vacate" hiding in there. That's vacate, go, be gone, get outta there, vamoose.

{ "Rocked in the cradle of the deep, I lay me down in peace to sleep."

~Emma Hart Willard

sleep

"If I felt any better I couldn't stand it."

–Brendan Behan

Get Enough

I bet you're not getting enough sleep. I rarely talk to anyone these days who says, "Oh, I'm so rested. I feel so good. I'm sleeping so well."

As the pace picks up, as we have more and more to do, one of the things we tend to give up is a proper night's sleep. That is if we even know what a proper sleep is. New studies suggest the accepted cultural wisdom that eight hours of sleep a night is the correct amount for an adult may be wrong.

Research indicates that we may be shortchanging ourselves at eight hours. Before time was structured, and we all had clocks to tell us when to go to bed and when to get up, most people probably slept about ten hours every night. Studies done with people who are considered "well rested," those who sleep a consistent eight hours every night, find they are more productive, more vital, more energetic and feel better once they begin sleeping ten hours every night.

> Sleep is an essential component of well-being.

Now stop throwing yourself down on the floor howling in despair. I'm not suggesting that you start sleeping ten hours a night tonight. I am suggesting, however, that you begin to pay more attention to how much sleep you get and to err on the side of more rather than less. And don't pretend that you can make up for the sleep that you lose during the week on the weekend—it's not true, you can't do it. All you do is disrupt your sleep patterns which can lead to insomnia and that's the opposite of the effect we're seeking.

If you're one of those people who functions perfectly on four hours a night, good for you. Leave the rest of us alone.

Sleep is an essential component of well-being. We try to outwit our need for it as if we can fool our bodies into thinking they really require less. Our bodies, however, are not like most of the people we know and are not easily fooled.

The only person you undermine when you're not well-rested is you. Unless you're a truck driver or an airplane pilot in which case you can undermine and compromise any number of people at the same time.

Avoid any obstacles to a good night's sleep. Coffee, tea, cola, and chocolate are all stimulants which activate the sympathetic nervous system preparing us for fight or flight. If you're doing any of these things before bed it will certainly have an impact on the quality of your sleep. And if you want to lower your stress level in general, I'd suggest eliminating these four substances totally. Cola and chocolate in particular are such staples of most people's diets that we never consider that they might be contributing to our stress, and the ads for these products sure won't tell you.

Noise disrupts your sleep, even if you sleep through it. Begin to pay attention to the noise levels in or around your bedroom. Find ways to reduce or mask as much of the noise as possible. Don't go to sleep with the television on. Not only is it noisy but you're feeding data directly into your subconscious.

Rock 'n' roll is great. So is acoustic guitar. But not right before you go to bed. Music has a powerful effect on your nervous system. You are what you hear. Studies show that certain music has a calming effect on the body. Baroque music is often used for relaxation and concentration because it has a rhythm that approximates the beat of a relaxed heart (about sixty beats per minute). If you're having trouble sleeping, or falling asleep, try putting on something Baroque rather than Marilyn Manson.

The news! Avoid it before bedtime in any form. That means no newspapers, no TV, and no radio before bed. The news is emotionally stimulating and, because in this society most of the news is bad news, it increases our anxiety and tendency to worry. Not the road to a good night's sleep.

Lack of exercise can make it more difficult to sleep. But don't exercise right before bedtime. Your body says "sleep" but your mind's in high gear. This is the time to use breathing techniques, but don't do them in bed. Make sure you are relaxed and ready to fall asleep before getting into bed.

> "No day is so bad it can't be
> fixed with a nap."
>
> ~Carrie Snow

Take a Nap

Once you've mastered a good night's sleep, you can move on to advanced sleeping, affectionately known as napping. I don't recommend napping to anyone who isn't sleeping well at night; it will only make things worse. However, for those of you sleep-like-a-log folks, napping is a terrific addition to your sleep repertoire.

Naps are, by definition, short. Men seem to be very good at power naps, which are ten minutes or less. A good nap, however, is between twenty and thirty minutes. If you're napping for an hour or more, you're really sleeping and it will most likely take you a good amount of time to fully wake up. Long naps also will influence your sleep schedule and will make you more in need of a nap the next day.

When I nap, I set a timer for twenty-five minutes and get up when it goes off. Sometimes I sleep, sometimes I doze, sometimes I just rest. (When I just rest, I pretend to myself that I meditated.) Regardless of what has actually transpired, I feel rested and much more alert.

Lose yourself to a snooze. It's a luxury.

"Insanity is doing the same thing over and over again, but expecting different results."

~Rita Mae Brown

stop the madness

Television

Turn off your TV. Yes, I know you don't want to do this. You love your TV. You need your TV. You only watch PBS and the news.

Stop with the excuses. We've all the read the statistics and most of us are watching too much TV. Studies have shown that people do not feel more relaxed or satisfied after watching TV. So, if you think you're doing it to relieve stress, it's not working.

The good news is that if you stop watching TV, you'll have time to do all the things you've read about in this book that you were sure you didn't have time to do. You'll have time to do yoga or dance or sing. You'll have time to talk to each other, play a game with the kids, or read aloud. You'll have time to go for a walk or sit outside and look at the stars. You can write in your journal or color in your coloring book. You can put something wonderful together with Tinkertoys. You can listen to Bach, Beethoven, or Bon Jovi. You can have a life.

If you won't turn off the TV, try this.

Turn it on at the start of the program you're going to watch and turn it off as soon as the program is over. Don't channel surf. Who needs to watch sound bites of nothing?

Don't watch the news before you go to bed. I'd say don't watch the news at all, but many people tell me they are addicted to the news. I don't understand why people watch something that creates so much stress for no reason. But still we watch. So, if you must watch, don't do so right before you go to bed. The last thing you do at night is what your unconscious picks up on. Fill yourself with relaxing, soothing images. We want sleep to be a time of rest, not wrestling.

I don't watch the news at all, I don't read the newspaper, and I don't listen to the news on the radio. Amazingly, I seem to know what I need to know to function in the world. I seem to hear about the weather enough to know if I should wear a sweater or carry an umbrella. People talk or I can look out the window. I don't know about every gang episode, every murder, every case of child abuse, every fire, or every drug bust. And I'm just fine with not knowing, thank you very much.

I gave up the news about five years ago. I thought my life had enough noteworthy things of its own and that I didn't require outside overload. I have never missed it at all. I do know people who claim they are addicted to the news and couldn't give it up no matter what it does to them. I suggest that any time you use the word "addicted" in reference to anything, it's time to give it up.

For now, if you're an avid news watcher, try not watching it before bed for the next three weeks. See if you notice any difference in your sleep or your attitude. I bet you will.

For the rest of you, turn it off.

> *"Tell me what you eat and I will tell you what you are."*
>
> ~Anthelme Brillat-Savarin

Sugar and Caffeine

You have to know that sugar and caffeine are not good for you. If you don't and you do a lot of either one, stop for two days and see how you feel. It's called withdrawal, and it's nasty. I know. I've been there.

Using these two substances is the equivalent of doing drugs. Your habit is just socially acceptable.

Both sugar and caffeine create "jolts" in your body. Plus, an increased amount of sugar can lead to mature-age-onset diabetes, which means that essentially we're sugaring ourselves to death. For a more detailed look at what sugar does, read *Sugar Blues* by William Duffy. Not that we're slow learners, but the book was written in 1976. Once you read it you will either stop doing sugar altogether or you'll do a lot less. Hopefully, if nothing else, you'll stop giving it to your children. When I see small children drinking soft drinks I want to cry—so much sugar in such small bodies. Yes, sugar tastes great and so does all the fabulous stuff made from it. But it's deadly and silent. Well, actually not so silent.

I can remember the time my friend Cathy Duarte, an amazing baker, made a chocolate cake for Steven's birthday. (You remember Steven, he cries at funerals.) It was like nothing I had ever tasted in my life, so rich, so chocolatey, a true slice of heaven. After half a slice each, we were all laughing helplessly about nothing at all. We couldn't do any more work that day because none of us could think. It felt like the top of my head was coming off and my eyes were bugging out. I'll never forget it. Steven took that cake home to his children. What are we thinking when we do these things?

I wish I could tell you how many mornings I've awakened feeling like there was no point to my life and no reason to go on. Given the opportunity at that moment, I would evaporate. At some juncture, during all of my death-wish thinking, I realized that I had eaten ice cream, cake, or some other heavily sugared thing the day before. I heaved a great sigh and realized I'm not really suicidal, I'm just sugarcidal. These days I can laugh about it, know that I'll feel dumpy for two days, and go on about my business. However, until I understood that sugar was controlling my will to live, I had some pretty scary days, weeks, and an occasional month.

I don't have sugar very often anymore. It's not worth it to me. I feel lucky to have such a clear indicator. The message, "Hey, this isn't good for you," could hardly be more blatant. Still, once in a while I'm at someone's house and there's something fabulous being served and I can't resist. (Excuse me, I mean I don't resist.)

And in the morning I wake up believing there is no point to my life.

Everyone knows about the crash at the end of the caffeine. It's why people have to have more coffee or more cola as the day goes on. And it's getting worse—now they're making carbonated drinks with extra caffeine! I love it when people tell me caffeine doesn't affect them. I'd like to see them about thirty-six hours after they haven't had any. Actually, I wouldn't like it at all. I've had caffeine withdrawal headaches and they're awful. I don't miss caffeine at all and you won't either—but prepare yourself for a seven-to ten-day withdrawal process.

> A constant roller coaster of stimulants is not life-enhancing.

I actually took a week off when I kicked caffeine. I had tried to give it up a number of times, but felt so awful at work I'd wind up going back to it. Think about how you can take good care of yourself for the time it takes to get the caffeine out of your system once and for all.

And then there's chocolate, the magical blend of sugar and caffeine. Need I say more?

Putting your body through a constant roller coaster of stimulants is not life-enhancing or stress-reducing. If you want to feel better, throw out the coffee, the soft drinks, and the chocolate. Yes, it's a terrible sacrifice for an American. I understand completely.

> *"You can't have everything.*
> *Where would you put it?"*
>
> ~Steven Wright

Stuff

Where did we get this predilection for "stuff"? What is this greedy, needy thing we all have? My friend Marye Gail Harrison has just finished reading a book called *How To Want What You Have* by Timothy Miller. Miller's premise is that Americans have some kind of accumulation addiction and that everything we do is about getting more stuff. He believes we're hardwired to always want more. I wonder how this happened to so many of us and I wonder why.

In my own life, I'm aware that my stuff holds me down. It keeps me aware that I have to earn a particular amount of money to support it all, that I'm unable to leave my present locale quickly or easily because my stuff's all here, that I can't just "get out of town" and disappear— someone would be looking for me wanting to know what to do with all of this stuff.

Do I need all this stuff? I doubt it. There's stuff in the

attic in boxes that's a mystery to me, but I do know that I've lived here for a year without it. If I went and opened the boxes, I would probably find things that I felt I had to have, but I've done nicely without them for twelve months so who am I kidding?

Take a look around you. What do you see? How much of it is necessary? Why do you have it? Does it serve any purpose? How much "weight" does it create in your life?

More than that, I want you to think about the stuff you don't have yet that you're still yearning for. Is it really necessary? Can the money be used for something else instead? How about paying off the mortgage, feeding a hungry child, or saving the rainforests?

What would your life be like if you had less stuff? What would your stress level be like?

There are suddenly a lot of books on the market about simplifying our lives. This tells me that we are starting to feel quite burdened by all the stuff, but not sure what to do about it. Take a look at *Simplify Your Life* by Elaine St. James.

Go throw something out, and see if you can refrain from buying anything new for a week. I know, I know—it's a major challenge.

> "One way to get high blood pressure is to go mountain climbing over molehills."
>
> ~Earl Wilson

Worry

How much of our lives do we spend worrying about things over which we have absolutely no control? And, I mean none. Like what the management of the company is going to do next and how that will affect our pensions, our careers, or whether or not we even have jobs tomorrow. How much time do you spend on that? Well, what's the worst that can happen? You'll lose your job or your pension or change careers. Until it happens, you can't do much about it (unless, of course, you want to get ahead of the game and make something happen, but that's different than worrying about it). So why spend any time on it? What's the point and what's the outcome? Not much of anything based on my experience. Worrying is one of the biggest wastes of time and talent.

I know many smart people who spend considerable time worrying. Worrying is always about things in the future that we can't do anything about at the moment.

Or, things that aren't ours to do. So, what's the point? I mean, why would you spend any time today on something that's not happening right now, when right now is all you've got?

I recently conducted a workshop just after I had read an article on meteors, the gist of which was that the "big one" is definitely coming. No one knows when it will hit—it could be fifty years or fifty thousand—but when it hits, we're history. I asked people what they thought about it and they came up with all kinds of things to worry about. My biggest concern is that when it hits I want to be having a great time, owe people a lot of money, and be thirty pounds overweight. Talk about a way to take care of a bunch of things at once.

> Until it happens, you can't do too much about it.

I can't do anything about meteors. They are not within my control. So I want to be having a great time from now right up until the big one takes us out. Don't you? (Unless you're a scientist who specializes in meteors and you want to spend your time trying to figure out how to stop it before it takes us out. That's great, but have a good time while you're working on it. Don't let the last five seconds find you pulling your hair out and wailing.)

What are we waiting for? What do you believe you're gaining by not having a good time? By not being happy and relaxed in your life right now?

I have a magnet on my refrigerator that says, "Relax—nothing is that important." And it's true. Nothing is. Nothing. Relax.

> *"Some mornings it just doesn't seem worth it to gnaw through the leather straps."*
>
> ~Emo Phillips

Take Your Pick

One of the places I get into trouble all of the time is when I'm working with groups of corporate employees and I talk about choice. No one has hit me yet, but I think it's just a matter of time. There is an incredible belief operating among hordes of people that they are working for someone or something and it's not of their choosing or their responsibility.

Let's consider that. You get up in the morning at a time that will allow you to get where you're going when you're supposed to be there. You go through your hygiene routine, maybe you exercise, perhaps you eat a little something. You get yourself and whomever you feel you have responsibility for out of the house and on the way to wherever you're all going. You get to work, park the car, and go in. Who forced you to do this?

To immediately feel better about going to work every day, simply remember that it's a choice you make, every single morning. If you hate it, I don't know why you choose it, but you do. This would be a good thing to think about. "I hate my job. Why do I choose to go there every day?" For a beginning journal entry, this is a doozy.

I was once in a group that did wind up on their feet shouting when we talked about choice. They were having none of it. They worked for their company because they had to, not because they chose to. So after I got them to calm down, we talked through why they did come to work every day if they felt it wasn't a choice. Many of them said they came to work because they had a mortgage to pay (that's usually the number one answer, by the way). Some said it was because they had children in college and were paying huge tuition bills. My next question was, "Okay, fine. Who makes you come here every day?" This confused them and they blundered around, but eventually they did have to admit that no one made them come. They came because they wanted to. Maybe they came because they wanted to pay for something or live in a particular place, but, in the end, they did agree that they made a choice.

Everything we do is a choice.

Why were they so unclear about their choices? My friend Kaitryn Wertz at Special Solutions, Inc. explains it this way: When you first learn to drive a car you are very aware of putting your foot on the gas and then moving it to the brake. You are conscious of signaling for a turn and what lane you're driving in. After you've been driving for twenty years there's little or no thought process for putting on the brakes or changing lanes. You know how to do it. You know where things are and it just happens.

If I told most people that every time they use the brakes it's a choice, they'd probably laugh at me. But logically, it is. It's just a choice that doesn't take up any of our mental space anymore. There are lots of things that happen to us that are like this.

Sometimes I choose to be angry without any sense that it was a choice. It happens so fast I don't see how it could be a choice. The truth is, that it's probably a situation where I've chosen anger before and probably many times before. I'm so good at choosing anger in that kind of situation, I'm no longer even aware of the choice. It's just like putting on the brakes—I just do it. Knowing this allows me to decide whether I want to stay angry or move on to something else. My "snits" get shorter and shorter. For me, this is a blessing.

When we begin to take responsibility for our lives by recognizing that everything we do is a choice, we liberate ourselves. Being clear that our lives are made up of the choices we make allows us to throw out any shred of "victim." If we are making choices and we don't like them, then, hallelujah, we can make different choices that we like better. And if those don't work out, we can choose again. We can always choose again. Isn't that great!

People argue with me about this all the time. But if you think about it, in your heart of hearts, you know it's true. It's really just common sense.

What are you choosing? How does it work in your life? What kinds of choices would you like to make? What keeps you from making them?

Choose again.

{ "People are just about as happy as they make up their minds to be." }

~Abraham Lincoln

the power of happiness

Why aren't you happy all the time? What are you waiting for? What do you believe is outside you that would be the thing that would make you happy? How many times have you gotten the "thing" and found that after the initial rush, you weren't any happier than before? In fact, you may be less happy.

Our happiness resides within us. The great mistake most of us make is looking for it somewhere outside of ourselves. If I decide that it takes another person to make me happy, then I have just put my happiness into someone else's hands. Do I really expect that another person will do exactly what I want him or her to do so that I can be happy? Maybe. And that's why so many of us are disappointed in our relationships.

The only person I want to determine my happiness is me. I don't want it in your hands or my boss's hands or my son's hands or the electrician's hands. If any of them have it, then I'm at their mercy and they each have their own lives to think about and their own happiness. I can't expect them to put my happiness first. Only I can do that.

When I'm happy, I'm productive. When I'm happy, I pass it on. When I'm happy, my happiness ripples out all around me and has an effect on others around me. I think my happiness can actually make a difference in other people's lives.

If you think happiness is a silly goal, think again. Consider what your life is like when you are really happy and what it's like when you're not.

Which do you prefer?

"Nature seems to have implanted gratitude in all living creatures."

~Samuel Johnson

an attitude of gratitude

After you've tried everything in this book, there will come a day when none of it matters and you feel like it's the end of the line or the rope or whatever. This is when we all need to put on an attitude of gratitude.

An attitude of gratitude isn't difficult. It just requires one second of willingness and that may take some doing on an end-of-the-rope day. But if you can find that one second, here's what you can do:

Be grateful for something. One thing. I don't care what it is. Eyesight. Sunshine. Ice Cream. Email. Breathing.

And then be grateful for one more thing. Just one.

And then just one more, just one.

And then one more. And, c'mon, c'mon—one more.

If you have the strength, jot them down on paper. Watch how the list grows and grows. Flowers, color, movement, soft rain, thunder, a child's laughter, a certain song, whipped cream, radio.

Whatever you don't have, whatever is ailing you, is far outnumbered by the things you do have. Right now. This minute.

Stay with one more thing and one more thing until the end of the rope is no longer where you are. Then add a deep breath to each one more thing until you feel calm.

And then go color for a while.

"It often happens that I wake at night and begin to think about a serious problem and decide I must tell the Pope about it. Then I wake up completely and remember that I am the Pope."

~Pope John XXIII

the last hurrah

In the end, when all is said and done, there is you and your life.

What works for other people becomes totally irrelevant if it doesn't work for you. If nothing you've read here jumps out as your answer to quick relief, keep looking. There is something that will work for you. In fact, think for a moment right now and find out what it is. If you get an I-don't-know answer, then guess. Guessing has a tendency to be amazingly accurate.

More than anything, find ways to enjoy your life as it is. Today. In this instant. Whatever you don't like, change. It's the beauty of being human. We get to change our minds. We get to choose again. And we know how to laugh.

Go find someone to laugh with, blow some bubbles, put together a puzzle. Sing a little song. Smile a lot. Give a hug.

All of us are better for it when you feel good. If you can't or won't do it for yourself, do it for the rest of us!

Lois Levy, M.S., is an organization development consultant specializing in executive and leadership development. An expert storyteller and workshop leader, Lois has developed a unique one-on-one executive coaching model for senior managers out of her first-hand experience with downsizing, mergers, takeovers, and reorganization. She consults with Fortune 500 senior managers and staff to significantly increase their effectiveness. As a single mother and a corporate executive at CIGNA Corporation, Lois learned how to keep her own life balanced and taught the people who worked with her the value of having balance in their lives. Her holistic approach extends well beyond strategic plans and shareholder equity. Many of her clients believe they have had their lives restored to them along with the bottom line.

Lois Levy lives in South Florida.